T0147599

American Socialism? It Is What It is

American Socialism?

It Is What It is

Terry L Ursini

iUniverse, Inc.
New York Bloomington

American Socialism? It Is What It is

iUniverse books may be ordered through booksellers or by contacting:

iUniverse
1663 Liberty Drive
Bloomington, IN 47403
www.iuniverse.com
1-800-Authors (1-800-288-4677)

Because of the dynamic nature of the Internet, any Web addresses or links contained in this book may have changed since publication and may no longer be valid. The views expressed in this work are solely those of the author and do not necessarily reflect the views of the publisher, and the publisher hereby disclaims any responsibility for them.

ISBN: 978-1-4502-5237-9 (sc)
ISBN: 978-1-4502-5148-8 (ebook)

Printed in the United States of America

iUniverse rev. date: 08/04/2010

For the American Individual,
may you live free, with minimal government interference,
with justice for all, with honesty, with integrity of person, and
with the ability to work hard for a fair days pay without being
subjected to selfish efforts of Madison Avenue.

Contents

Introduction

Is this a book really talking about the United States of America? Shocking as it may seem the answer is, yes. It seems the advent of the computer age, the impending retirement of the baby boomers and the "recession" all came together to create a scenario where institutional socialism is being forced on a generation of workers. People became expendable and computer systems became the new work horse. It would be great to say this was just a natural outgrowth of the ability to operate, process and execute at very high levels. Yet, the question must also be asked, are we our brother's keeper, or is our brother the problem and not the solution?

How do you grow a community under the process management style of management without the leveling forces of organized labor, and in the face of globalization, the new world economy? Can an individual actually work for some company and expect a fair wage for a day's work, or has management/shareholder greed created and maintain the new working poor, the hourly worker? What is the role of government in insuring the rights of the individual or are we repeating the robber baron era of the early 1900's, where it is the President who could talk loudly and carry a big stick? Where were you when you lost it all, or where were you when the subtle shifts by management made you less important, almost obsolete. Fascinating questions. This book sets out to explain what has happened to the American lifestyle, the American worker and what the we all need to think about.

As time went by, talking about writing this book became very interesting. Many of the people that were introduced to this concept, stared in total shock, then stated how they knew things were different, had seen the changes, and just never put the parts together to see the total impact on their lives. They all seemed to express the same sentiment, that the parts do not seem harmful, yet as a whole, this is just wrong. The next thought was, now that the total impact is known, what do we need to do to change this? It was amazing how the solution was not even considered, yet there is a situation that needs a solution. When some of the suggested solutions were offered, you could see the wheels turning and the potential impact of this book grew larger.

This book is not written to change history, the impact of this book will hopefully be the awakening of people to the need to remain and maintain the status as an American individual. We are not sheep-people, we have no need to be in compliance with every system in order to obtain customer service, and surely we do not need to over pay management to obtain a better product.

Special thanks to Joyce Pipkin, a great friend.

So it begins............

Where Did This Come From ?

Where did the title of this book come from? American socialism, how crazy an idea; most people will say it cannot happen here. As sick as it may be, the process has slowly and effectively been taking over company after company, government after government. The process is not finished. Whether it continues or not, is up to us.

First though, let us explore the roots of this process. Process management became a management tool and training method in the late 1990's. By itself, the process management axiom of "manage the process, not the people" seems innocent. Having a management style in which the process is the main focus seemed like just another theme of the year in which many companies would push, only to abandon it later for something new. What changed this time was a small item that was beginning to be so effective and widespread no one knew the impact it would have on the business and government systems. The computer was taking over and getting more and more powerful each and every month. It was the merger of the idea and the technology that took a simple process to such extreme levels.

The computer possessed something that management systems never had before, large memory and instant duplication. In other systems, after the management meeting and implementation of the new process, people gradually tweaked the new process, with the end result a blend of the system and the real world response from people. This time the computer had the ability to stop the tweaking of the process. Suddenly, management found that a new system could be started, with the end result being very close to the startup version. No longer could people change, modify, accept or reject the system in bits and pieces. Suddenly, the computer version was "the" version. Now the new threat came into play as management started pushing back at the employees stating, "what part of what is on the screen do you not understand" and even more sinister than that was the new, " read the screen, follow the instructions or you will be charged with failure to follow instructions." Now, workers no longer had a choice in the style and version of the work to be performed. As it is written, so it must be followed. The marching orders were sent and total acquiescence was required and expected.

WOW, does this really work? Upper management quickly saw that this works perfectly in customer service operations. Long an area of concern, many managers felt the gains from sales were always given away by the customer service side of the business. Management could reduce the size of customer service operations, and insure their words were followed explicitly, simply by creating written operations instructions. These instructions could easily be made available on all computers, serving as instructions of what the operator could and could not do. Anything not written was not allowable, no concessions, altering or bending of the rules. As it is written, is all that is allowable. All the operator had to do was follow the written word, and everyone would be happy.

Welcome to the world of the SOP, standard operating procedures. Management could control entire departments, control entire divisions, by insisting the computer written word was to be followed, no questions asked. Supervisors were only there to insure the written word was followed. Supervisors no longer needed the authority for any function except for insuring all employees follow what was on the screen. It started slowly, one function after another, yet the results began to show. Upper management quickly noticed they had a new level of control, total control. The employees had no opinion, nor was the employee opinion allowed. They were employees, management runs the company, management makes the rules. What part of read the screen and the command to follow instructions did the employee not understand, and if you cannot read and follow instructions, well then maybe this was not the job for you. Control, maximum control, behavioral modification at it's finest. No longer did management need to worry about what the employees were or were not doing or saying. If an employee did not follow the written rules precisely, well then the actions of the employee did not implicate or commit the company as the actions of the employee were not authorized. This was just too simple, why did this take so long to discover? The process had begun, it worked, it saved money, it increased productivity, it showed areas where there were too many employees. Nirvana, control and the ability to cut costs was a businessman's dream. How about the dream of a bureaucrat?

The bureaucrat's main purpose in life is to have a system that keeps them busy, re-enforces the need for their employment and requires no action of their own to maintain.

So how does keep busy equate to fulltime employment and when there is no productive or necessary work involved?

To bureaucrats, a system that gives them the same tasks daily is important, as their own self importance is derived from being vital to the organization. The role of gatekeeper is part and parcel of being "needed" by the organization. Bureaucrats do not understand the concept of working themselves out of a job by growing towards a greater position or a new job. They only understand they are doing a function that no one can perform as well as they can. Until they choose to seek an advancement or location change, the bureaucrats entire purpose is self preservation and survival. There are many "dead end jobs" that require a bureaucrat to process the same functions daily, a good example is vehicle registration. We need people to sit there and solve problems. Yet as career bureaucrats they seldom take the responsibility of their work as anything that important. This leads to an uninspired worker just filling the hours without much joy and enthusiasm. Maybe we ask too much, yet whether you are a waitress or a clerk, you are being paid to perform work, and most Americans expect good customer service from those who are in the position to serve the customer.

The SOP orders were now able to be issued, followed by all and applicable to business and government. The slight problem of a system that ignores the human rights of the individual was not even addressed. This new found power was just too much fun to think about real people. This new system was deemed as a perfect solution to handling any and all employee issues. Employers no longer are required to "deal" with the issues of the employee, as that depth of knowledge of an individual is now seen as a private matter, having no place in the workplace. The employee is hired to perform a job as described by the SOP; dealing with employee issues is not part of the SOP. The human factor was removed from the worksite. Robots, with no real lives, were expected to show up, follow the SOP and then go home, happy that they had a low paying job, where they were not required to think, just read the screen and follow the instructions on the screen. Whoever thought of such a robotic, demeaning, personality less system,...enter Senator Sarbanes and Senator Oxley.

Sarbanes-Oxley

Sarbanes-Oxley. (SOX) Just repeal it and hope we can forget it.

The Sarbanes-Oxley Act of 2002, is a federal law enacted on July 30, 2002 as a reaction to scandals of large publicly traded companies. This law has crept into more companies than originally intended, including government entities and governments. The extent of this law is not what became the important impact of this law. Sarbanes-Oxley became the catalyst for a centralized socialistic form of control. Whether or not this was the original intent will probably be known by insiders and think tanks only.

The law had all the good intentions of all good laws, yet when handed over to the bureaucrats they saw their chance to rule the world. This law was created to manage the risk of a shareholder in a way that would prevent another collapse of a company, caused by the use and/or misuse of company/shareholder assets or equity. Enron, Tyco are the poster children for the creation of this legislation. As this law was pushed on many public traded companies, a new job was created with the title of Compliance Officer.

Suddenly, this law required all public traded companies to prove the assets of the company were spent only for the business purposes of the company. Simple enough, yet the underside of this law was in the proof. Certain words became the rules of this simple law. Compliance, prove, authorized, reasonable, expected, certify, understood, and more took on new meanings. Entire new compliance departments needed to be created, at a expense to the company, not the government, to insure the intent and meaning of this law were established and maintained. Simple enough, yet no one saw what this simple law would ultimately mean to every American.

"...the responsibility of management for establishing and maintaining an adequate internal control structure and procedures for financial reporting." Title IV of the act, consisting of nine sections, with this quote from Wikipedia explaining the basic essence for the creation, promotion and maintenance of what has become increasingly a centralized socialistic system.

The freedom to make judgment calls, good or bad, success or failure, the basic right of a manager to manage, is stripped away by the act. Establishing and maintaining set for a level of command and control that eroded and/or removed the freedoms enjoyed by corporations and eventually the customers.

When this part of the law was turned over to the bureaucrats, the subtle changes regarding the type and level of control became obvious. This level of authority was assigned to a lower level employee and a new empire was created. Suddenly, this new SOX Compliance Manager learned this position controlled the entire company through the constant and prying eyes of Sarbanes Oxley. The old saying of whoever controlled the purse strings of the kingdom ran the kingdom no longer worked. The new ruler of the realm was the one who interprets the law and keeps us in compliance is the true ruler of the realm. This resulted in the CEO, CFO, the entire Board of Directors were mere slaves to the SOX Compliance Manager. Why?

The words used by a compliance control department generally follow one rule. IF, there is a rule, law, provision, business practice or procedure; basically everything, becomes subject to full compliance with the letter of the rule, etcetera, AND the rules of SOX. IF, the rule, etcetera is not pertinent or needed then the entity must either follow the rule or remove it from the books. Example: A Nevada town had an old law on the books which required masks be worn by everyone while in the downtown area. Quaint, historical or not, SOX would require this be followed and enforced or repealed. IF the supposed rulers of the realm do not repeal the old or no longer applicable rules, then the entity must be in full compliance with the very letter of each and every rule. Wear a mask or repeal the law.

This requirement to be in full compliance with the rule or law was always backed up by the bureaucrats dream statement; "What part of the written word do you not understand?" The tables were turned. Compliance became the driving force, regardless of cost, as companies rushed to be in compliance. The Board of Directors quickly became a powerless shell. No decision, expenditure or project could proceed without a complete compliance review. Managers everywhere began receiving mandates to move toward complete compliance. These unfunded mandates flooded the field with the new standards for operating an American public company. Post this, insure that this new procedure is in place, sign this under strict penalty for any and all failure to comply. Personal and total accountability for everything was pushed out to the field.

Every employee has a new and unknown title, scapegoat. Webster's dictionary describes scapegoat as: " 2. a person or thing bearing the blame for others."

Any department and/or any employee was expected to be in compliance with the rules, or face the penalty for noncompliance. Any and all failure to follow the written word, whether understood or NOT, was not an acceptable result for the employee.
Here you can see the shift of responsibility from a system of actions that produce success or failure to employees who are now 100% liable and will be held accountable for every single letter in every single law or rule.

There was no explanation of this shift, there was no press release. The move forward into this socialistic control of the entity was just that , a quiet steady move for total control.
Labor did not see it coming, Management associations never understood the depth of this cancer, everyone felt that the published intent of the

law, to prevent abuse of financial assets, was a good idea. The call to repeal the law is not based on the intent of the law.

The law needs to be repealed as it establishes authority in an entity to a lower level of employee. This dumbing down of the system has a very unforeseen side affect, with every manager above the lowest level employee has no authority. Decisions cannot be made until they are reviewed by compliance control and deemed in compliance or not in compliance. A manager standing at a customer counter could not properly authorize a refund unless it was first established through the use of Compliance Control, and a written part of the standard operating procedures.

All decisions must be authorized, acceptable and approved in advance of the action. If the SOP clearly granted authority to an action, it is allowable, if there is a question regarding the intent or authority, then a personal decision by a manager or employee should not be made, as no one has the company or governmental authority to make such a choice. Only the Compliance Control Department could choose to change the SOP, or in the absence of a decision, no decision is the correct choice.

Was the expenditure of funds a documented application following the rules for requests approved in advance by an authority authorized to approve said expenditures? If all the "I's" were not dotted and the "T's" not crossed then the request could not proceed.

Paperwork and procedure, bureaucrats love this stuff. Bureaucrats could sit in their offices and receive the request and rule in compliance or not in compliance without accountability. SOX Managers were not accountable for any or all actions of any employee or rule of the company, they only had to decide if the item was in compliance or not. Ruling that a refund was in full compliance with the law did NOT mean the refund was authorized. Others were still required to step up and accept full responsibility for approving the request. What a position to be in. The Control Officer, the law, had added penalties and accountability to every action and inaction of a company, and INSURED that the law and/or Compliance Office was not accountable or responsible for anything more than a non binding ruling. This is sick, this is socialist type of control.

This is a centralized system of management where every item, rule, and action is performed or designed to protect the company or the government.

Process management became the rage in the late 1990's, it had been around for a while, yet there was one thing that kept any system from meeting critical mass. Under process management the mandate was issue from the high office, and there was hope that all the troops would fall in line. The problem of communication and message leak had always been around. You start a plan, release the plan then sit back and hope for results. Audits were performed to see who was doing what and where, yet the communication at the bottom always had a way of muting into something less than the order that was originally issued. Process management declared that as a manager you were to focus on the process and stop focusing on the employee. The employee had no opinion in the process, so why would management listen to the employee? If the main office would state we should all paddle up river, then the managers were to inform and create the system where everyone would be paddling in the same direction. Well, it is common knowledge of what really happened. The communication would mutate into something less than the original communication, with each location evolving the process into something along the general lines of the communication, just not the exact communication. To many this local version was the best way to go, as the local manager could perform as requested by the main office and still take care of the local people and the customer. Another issue was the fact that results were never assured, hard to report on, and at times questionable as to whether there were results at all. New management always came along with a learning curve and the original communication was mutated even more. People were part of the process, and even though process management was designed to manage the process, not the people, people were still part of the process. Then, there was the customer, The customer could care less about the process, they just have great expectation for results, results that pleased them regardless of cost or impact on the organization. As organizations became more sophisticated, there needed to be a tool that could remove people from the process, so that the organization could issue, monitor and review results in a timely basis. Enter the computer.

After the great Y2K process, most companies had entire departments set up to monitor, upgrade and maintain a growing computer network. Somewhere out there, process management collided with instant communication and Nirvana for the bureaucrat was formed. For the first time ever a communication could be issued by the main office and the message would arrive at all connected locations at the same time with the same impact. Better yet, no one could change, alter or modify the message. The message was received as sent. OK, so now what would happen after the email was opened and read?

Like normal humans, most wanted communication or push back regarding how this new rule would impact the local situation. The computer just sat there, the original message still on the screen, nothing had changed. Since the original message was sent from on high, the upper middle managers closest to the issuing office were told they could not allow any changes whatsoever from the message, as it was written, so shall it be done. Period. Period, again. Notice that change? Suddenly, the local manager had no authority, his boss had no authority. no one had any authority over the new message, except for the office of origin. Managers could call their boss as many did, only to find a new gate keeper had taken over and it was not the person they were talking to. The new gatekeeper was compliance. Without input, without comment, without alteration the new rules began to cascade through the computer crashing into the humans at the receiving end, with devastating results for humans. Managers were no longer in the position to manage their office; they now had to manage their office to the standards of the process, as it is written, so shall it be done. Who needs a manager? Anyone can read a computer screen, and follow the instructions, right? The local manager still had parts of the old process to consider, and the demands of the new systems. The manager became the perfect scapegoat, totally responsible and accountable, under penalty for failure and had no control over anything, except insuring the unit was in compliance with the decrees.

Along with messages going out in 100% perfect form as issued, now the main office could demand results immediately. These results started with a simple demand to reply that the message had been received, as part of the process was to insure someone at each location was hooked into being the responsible scapegoat for that location. Then the reporting requirements followed, as since we now know the message was sent perfectly, and received by the "accountable" manager, results or proof of compliance was the natural best step. Now the computer demands could say when local offices are to jump, how high, and then monitor the system for demanded results to see what really happened. Finally, process management had really started. With the aid of the computer, process management quickly took over as the premier management process.

For employees, the end was now in sight, their end. Main offices no longer had to consider local issues; everyone at every location was expected to read and comply. Call in branding insurance, now a customer could expect the same treatment at every location as every location was expected to be in full compliance with all standards. Once an office reported full compliance, then the numbers could be used to see how each office compared to the rest of the field. The vital few who reported bad numbers were soon bombarded with extra demands and pressure to meet the standard, no exceptions allowed.

Since everyone had received the same message, and everyone had reported, there was no reason for non compliance and no reason for bad numbers. Every office is required to meet standards. Employees, equipment, supplies, etc. would all be compared to the standard office with all cut to match the standard office regardless of local impact. Standards are standards, and every office should be required to perform to the exact same standard, compliance.

So, here we have a law called Sarbanes-Oxley, combining with a business system called process management, and at the speed of the new technology, the computer. Socialism and/or centralized management won, freedom was lost.

Is it wrong to use technology, process and law to run a business? No, not at all. It is wrong to forget that there are real people who still must perform to accomplish the tasks of the business. Many businesses seemed to forget this fact, with managers starting to react with such anger and frustration, and all employees becoming increasingly concerned about keeping their own job. People began to treat people as just another number, not as an asset of the company. Sarbanes Oxley had started as a way to protect the assets of the company, it ignored the human assets. The common feeling was that no employee was deemed as necessary, that all were expendable, that each employee was only as good as the last best performance provided by the employee for the company, and what was the employee doing for the company right now. The standards had been set, communicated, and reported back in compliance, nothing else and no one else mattered. It is what it is.

As Sarbanes-Oxley invaded more and more industries free people everywhere have begun to question this law. Most business just figure they need to comply so they step it up and fall into line. This is the correct thing to do to stay in compliance, it is not the only action item that should have been complied with. The question is "Who died on 9-11 that left the bureaucrats in charge?" As Americans reacted to the attack, one of the first cries that went out was how was this allowed to happen? Naturally, a government in power who just got caught with their proverbial pants down is going to respond like all well entrenched bureaucrats do, the finger is pointed outward and/or the call that there should have been a law to prevent this from happening. Yes, citizens' level of fear was raised, then when anger took over, the government began creating new laws and taking new freedoms usually not granted to a government that just failed. The difference here was the spin doctors were able to quickly and effectively divert the attention away from the administration's errors, to a policy of protection and let's go get them. Action, any action, seemed better than taking the blame. Homeland Security was created along with all the department's new laws and regulations and the incorporation of Sarbanes-Oxley became a natural step. The scenario was set, protect the public by requiring the public come into compliance with wide ranging action items that would be visual and impact everyone long enough and dramatically enough that the public would no longer focus their anger toward the government. The need for personal accountability through compliance became the action item. Americans all know and have experienced the prime example of this bureaucratic action in our airports. If, we hire a massive number of Transportation Aviation employees, require all passengers to prove who they are through the use of accurate documents, increase fees on all tickets to pay for this, adjust to any new found possible risks, like now requiring we take our shoes off, remove toothpaste, empty all pockets before walking through a machine, and many more items not listed here which are now required by all airlines, then the government could state that the government is performing the job of homeland protection. This process also establishes the outright frontal fact that the American people are not capable of protecting themselves from any and all threats both foreign and domestic. Here we have a government increasing the size and scope of government intervention into the personal lives of the citizens under the disguise of fulfilling the need to protect the citizenry.

As bureaucrats everywhere held their breath to see the reaction of the average American, the process began. This process should have stopped at the governmental need to provide protection, or included insurance and review that the personal freedoms of all Americans would be maintained. The perfect storm had arrived, and while the American public did not see it happening, the bureaucrats did. Welcome to the age of the controlling and all powerful bureaucrat, say goodbye to freedom. Planning had meet up with opportunity, and in the absence of resistance, brought on by fear. The compliance factor now began to spread everywhere. Banks became required to request for personal information, data for each transaction and set financial limits. Under the Bank Secrecy Act the government was required to mitigate the risk that America's enemies were transferring and raising cash. Notice that this time, instead of going after the bad guys, all actions to mitigate any and all risk, as originally stated in Sarbanes-Oxley, were now forced on any and all actions, on any and all companies and worst of all on all citizens. The government decided that in an effort to provide protection for all, the government would require pain be processed equally on all.

Sarbanes-Oxley rules for compliance with anything the government decide is necessary to be in compliance with quickly began to spread. If the federal government requires risk mitigation through personal accountability, then state government rules and regulations would be required to change to be in compliance with the new federal rules. The states fell in line, the cities fell in line, the towns, hamlets, even the dog catcher was no longer exempt from some form of compliance. Where would this go from here?

Welcome to Greed, excuse me, welcome to Pay for Performance or the bonus programs.

Somewhere out there an idea floated up, that now that employees were no longer needed, management was still temporarily required. To drive results and obtain expected performance, the idea of simply paying management a salary became out of date. Annual bonuses have always been around and now was the time to tie the bonus to performance in more industries. Hum...Preserve the system by paying incentives to those who might make trouble.

Patterns began to be noticed, not in one company, in many. Government after government began to replicate this new found power. Power originated through law, made effective and invasive by through effective application, which resulted in increased greed. Power of the written word being afforded the effect of absolute law, over and in many cases, inspite of common sense, and against the individual. Power to tell people, company divisions, customers, managers, everyone...being told the written word was the ultimate power, personal opinion or free thought no longer counted.

The Patterns

Business operational patterns began to develop that some will say erode personal freedom and others will say enhance personal freedom.

Is personal information necessary to conduct business between the business and the consumer? What type of information is actually personal and what portion is just common knowledge that can be found anywhere on the internet?

At this point a conversation with my brother still rings in my ears. Talking about the new systems he stated, " ...a person cannot hide anymore, everything is viewable, everything is more open than ever before." This brought forth thoughts regarding the ability to "hide" personal information, the need, or the emotional response. This modern world has most people performing banking online, buying and selling, listening to music or radio, watching television or video, making appointments and many other actions of the normal daily routine. Why would a person fear the distribution of personal information to a trusted company? Much of this information was already required by banks, mortgage companies, doctors' offices; it seemed that use of the online services made perfect sense. If everyone was vulnerable, why worry?

The collection and storage of personal information to be used solely for the transactions between the consumer and the company is a good practice. With the space issue becoming more and more expensive, a solution was needed. Most people have absolutely no problem with the transaction use only portion of data storage. Then the expansion of the web created a scenario where hackers could create problems. There were solutions to these attacks, so everything may have gone along just fine, sparing between the hackers and the companies, consumers obtaining benefits from retained data, the modern world was more open and risky, yet manageable.

The perversion of Sarbanes-Oxley and Compliance Procedures created something one would hope that no one wants. Sarbanes-Oxley was created to require the management of risk, from understanding what risks existed and to mitigate any potential loss associated with the risk, known and unknown. Through the accountability at a personal level, it was presumed that through legislated accountability there would be a reduction in the risk level. Accountability is not responsibility.

Whereas the information obtained and stored, a business to be accountable and responsible for the content, companies soon found they could mask the responsible use of the data under corporate talk saying, " use of and retention of this data is done to serve the customer better." So said the spider to the fly. The use of personal data in any way other than the original intent of the data collected is wrong on many levels.

As a company changes hands, there is always the change in the mission of the company. When a company changes the way the information is used, and does not seek the consumer's re-permission for this new use of the information, this is not right. If a consumer provides information to a company and knows up front that the information will be used for marketing purposes the consumer understands. It is when the purpose, style or the way the stored information is used, without contacting the consumer is where the problem starts. The right for the use of personal information should not be taken for granted that the customer agreed with and accepts the policies of the new company. Yet time and again, the consumer is not contacted when policy changes or a new company takes over. The protection and the notification of the consumer should be an important step.

You cannot hide, yet should everything be public knowledge? What part of the information requested before business can be transacted is really necessary. The ability to obtain information is now restricted by the security demands of the organization.

Name, address, birth date, SS#, number of kids, animals, do you like chocolate, how much are you willing to spend today, can you spend more; the questions asked by many companies are this ridiculous. Does a consumer have the right to access a company over the phone and ask a question without needing to prove who they are. The other question is that after supplying all this information which the company representative inputs into a computer, what happens to this information? How is the information used, how is it stored, who has access to this data base? When you access a web site, what information is being sent from your computer to the web site's computer without your knowledge? The ability to track and trace everyone and their transactions is quite incredible. Yet is the safety and security of the individual protected from use, or misuse, by anyone? A consumer must agree to privacy policies by clicking on a box that states the user has read and agrees with this policy. This action holds the user a hostage to agree with this legal policy which protects the company and allows use of the customer information, yet few read the policy.

The questions here is, must a consumer know all the legal, technical and mechanical properties of a product in order to purchase and use the product or service. The answer should be absolutely no. Lawyers have companies responding in this way to curtail the many unnecessary law suits. The consumer is faced with signing all rights away and being required to perform their due diligence to accept a good or service. No longer can a consumer just walk in and purchase a product without assuming all knowledge and liability for the use and misuse of the product. Basically, all a company wants to do is provide a good or service, and after serving the consumer, never be held accountable for any failure of the product or the service.

This leaves the consumer in the position of needing to know how to perform a plumbers job, the entire technical and operational use of a water heater, and all local laws and regulations, before the order to install a water heater can be issued. All legal ramifications from the decision to purchase and install a water heater are the sole responsibility of the consumer. The plumber does not want to be held responsible or warranty any part of the installation and accepts no responsibility for the type style and makeup of the parts installed. The parts manufactures does not want to be held responsible for any part of their manufactured product as the installer and the buyer is required to be perfect in the installation and use of the product, as any misuse or use viewed as misuse voids all warranties of the product. All the consumer wants is a new water heater, installed and working, and if it fails, someone to come out and replace or repair the problem unit. The plumber points the finger at the consumer or the product manufacturer. He was only accountable for installing the unit; anything that happens after that is not warranted by the plumber. The manufacturer states the product was fine when it left the factory, it must have been the plumber or the use by the consumer of the product in a way that the product was not designed for. Then the government demands their inclusion in the process by stating that prior to the installation a permit must be applied for and a fee paid. When the government is asked why, the answer is the product and installation needs to be checked for proper installation and current code compliance. The fee is applied to pay the cost of keeping the consumer in compliance, by providing this safety check service. When asked if the product fails can the government be sued along with the installer and the manufacturer? The answer is no. The government accepts no legal responsibility for any product or service, they are held harmless. So , why do we pay the fee? Because they can legally charge it. Everyone and every item wants to be held accountable, but no one wants to be responsible. The consumer is not protected, the consumer takes on the greatest risk, cannot mitigate this risk, and because of signed and agreed to policy statements has no recourse in the event of failure. The consumer is accountable and responsible for all. This is wrong. It should be the consumer who is in control and the companies who work for the consumer. This is not the pattern today.

Today, the companies work for themselves not for the consumer. The consumer is the problem, the company is the solution, a solution that comes with a total lack of risk.

Risk belongs to the consumer. The product supplier expects the consumer to state, oh product manufacturer, may I please purchase your product knowing that I the consumer take all responsibility for the installation, use and local law compliance and any other issue known or not known and may I pay the highest price possible to insure that your company can survive these hard economic times? Then the consumer needs to call the installer and ask, oh Mr. Plumber would you please find time, at your convenience and please use your acquired skills to install this product and I the consumer will guarantee that you the installer will not be held accountable or responsible for your work and I agree to pay you for each and every part installed and to accept the highest fee possible based on a book of standard fees that has nothing to do with the actual time spent on the installation, so if the book states the standard installation should take two hours and you finish the job in one hour, I the consumer will pay for two hours of your time. Then the government needs to come out and inspect the installation to justify the permit fee, and the consumer agrees to not only pay, but to be available and provide access to the property at the convenience of the inspector, regardless of the time the consumer must sit and wait for anyone to show up. The consumer time and money means nothing, only the company, service supplier and the government time and budget are important.

Tea Party. The division and diversion of the truths is part and parcel of this great sham. The Tea Party movement is wonderful, except the emotional responses of these attendees is spurred on by advantage seeking politicians. Yes, the issues that are stressed by the Tea Party movement are very important. It is in not understanding where and how these items became the problem is what is worrisome. Organizing the masses to follow a logical chain of thought , without divulging the real source of the problem, creates scapegoats and villains, does little to resolve the underlying issues. Health care reform is a hot topic at these meetings. Yet, little is said about the minimum wage that does not allow an individual minimum wage earner from actually affording health insurance. This creates a scenario where tax payers are covering the cost of insurance by subsidizing the employer who is not paying a livable wage. To stress that government should not be part of health care reform, that people are responsible to obtain their own health coverage, is ignoring the other side of the issue. Both sides need to be reviewed, and underlying laws that increase costs, like Sarbanes-Oxley need to be brought into the search for a reasonable solution. If paying a minimum wage allows the wage earner to qualify for social services, like food stamps, subsidized health care, and/or fall below the federal government poverty level, then all that is accomplished is taxpayers are subsidizing businesses. Basic wages and benefits should be provided by employers, with any and all enhancements paid by the employee. To ignore both sides does nothing to resolve the basic problem, do the wages actually meet or exceed the cost of living? Here private companies jump to pay people less, with no benefits, stating they are accountable only for the survival of their company, and not responsible for the education, social or personal needs of the employee. Company's just want to use, abuse and then refuse to be responsible for the social environment they helped create.

It is submitted once again:

Drama Politics:

Organizing the masses to follow a perceived logical chain of thought, without divulging the real source of the problems, creates scapegoats and villains, does little to resolve the underlying issues.

Being angry enough to get involved is great, IF it does not blind the individual from common sense judgments'. A certain political party stated that if the voter did not know the candidates the voter should stay home. This attempt to control the vote by belittling the voter, thus potentially reducing the number of votes needed to win does not help the entire issue of voter apathy or knowledge. Yes certain voters do not know all the candidates or issues, all voters should still be encouraged to get out and vote. To state that if you do not know-do not go, is just another way of voting for potentially the wrong candidate or issue. It is this win at all costs, through whatever means possible that has a potential of creating or electing people for the wrong reasons. Sure, we disagree with certain votes cast by the elected, we disliked our parents too, yet we lived in their house and under their rules. At least with politicians we can vote them out every few years, please vote with conviction, not from a drama induced frenzy. If drama causes a person to vote, then the issues meant nothing, and the vote was controlled and exhorted by the producer of the drama. We are not lemmings, ready to jump off a cliff because of drama, Americans know that strong responsible leadership does not mean we will always agree with every direction or decision made by the elected. Drums should not lead one to vote, quiet old common sense, determination and understanding will always produce the desired results.

No one wants to think that all political decisions are "my way or the highway" and no one likes to compromise. Yet, there must be discussion, without yelling; talk, without interruption; points of view, with acceptance-which does not mean approval; and time to ponder on what is best for all, not what is best for one side or the other. Ideas need to be floated, with time to grow, prosper or die, yet ideas need that free space. The new Right in America when compared to radical segments of foreign governments, have many of the same attributes. We all must be careful on how we defend democracy. After the yelling, campaigning, cartoons, jokes, signs, commercials, and opinions; we will all wake up tomorrow in America, the land of the free. The acceptance of diversity of person and of ideas is essential.

Marketing or Targeting?

Marketing to each and every customer based on the concept that each customer is a marketing opportunity, where each customer needs to be offered a good or service at each visit, is an attempt to get more money out of the customer. This total lack of respect for the consumer creates the scenario where the customer becomes the victim. If the customer says yes to the automatic consistent bombardment of the marketing department, the profits roll in and the customer generally buys something they did not intend to purchase when the customer entered the establishment. Business requires each employee to state mandatory corporate talk to suggest to the customer that more goods and services are available just by saying yes. This is the vocal version of the emotional buys, the spontaneous buy and/or the add on has always been part of retail marketing. While the customer is standing there why not sell, sell, sell? The reason that this has become a disrespectful addition to the retail experience is that in place of an occasional sales pitch, now the customer receives the canned corporate talk each time every time regardless of how many times the customer says no. The question is asked, how long can the consumer continue to spend at marketing inspired levels, while earning minimum wages, before the customer cannot come back for the basic good or service, let alone the marketed additions?

Wall Street Madison Avenue marketing states they are responsible for selling the products, the customers are responsible to know their own spending level.

Yes, that is true. So what can consumers do to control their spending and not respond to the marketing of corporate America. The good customers must do what good customers have always done when treated with a lack of dignity and respect. Good customers just go away. First remember you are in complete control, so buy what you want and realize that you are being sold to, regardless of what type of business you visit. Find businesses that appreciate your visit, that refrain from the robotic sales pitch provided to each and every customer, at every single visit. Prepare yourself to say No. The selling does not end with the clerk, now the selling is being included when using a debit/credit card, as a screen pops up in the card process asking if the customer wishes to donate to a cause championed by the store. Today this selling seems to be limited to charitable causes, yet are we being trained by good intentions to respond positively to corporate greed in the future. Yes, the customer needs to be aware and say no to the words spoken, just as the consumer must be aware and read the fine print, the benefits being offered are not for your good, they represent the greed of the company, a marketing attempt for the good of the company.

Pay for Performance

Pay for performance. Whatever happened to a salary or a basic wage? Somewhere out there a foundation determined that if a bonus program was created then a company could recruit and keep better people. The understanding was that if there were standards of performance that any performance exceeding these standards should be compensated.

Realtors have always had this incentive, if they want a bonus they need to focus and sell a higher priced property. Here the incentive was, work for it.

Wall Street has had a bonus program forever it seems, so why is there so much concern regarding the bonus program now?

The process changed when the program was spread across many industries from public utilities, restaurants and even government agencies. Now, people that never received a bonus before were required to perform in order to receive this extra payment. Notice the word extra.

An example is a school district that could not fund a larger salary and accepted an outside bonus payment from private enterprise as a way to enhance the pay package. This was done to attract higher qualified individuals to the job, the district felt that money was needed to compete with larger districts.

Government bonuses were offered as a way to compensate for higher performance.

The problems with this new look at a old process came from many areas. One area was when you sell a $100,000 home a realtor could net $3,000.00 and like wise on a $1,000,000 home sale, the net could be $30,000.00. Here the customer knew in advance the exact amount of the commission based on the percentage agreed to at the time of listing. There generally is no problem.

When Wall Street bonuses began to hit $1 billion, people on Main Street started to wonder, how are they paying this amount, where is the money coming from and am I paying for this? The number had reached the ouch factor, where the numbers were so big people began to suspect there was a problem whether or not there was a problem.

A public utility paid their CEO a bonus of $2,000,000.00 regardless of the fact that this was a state franchise, which means it was a government allowed monopoly for this service. The rate payers have no choice or opportunity to take their business elsewhere, they are stuck with the pay package policy created by the publicly traded corporation.

Then there were those famous Golden Parachutes, where retiring executives or fired executives walked away from corporations with millions and millions of dollars. Agreed to or not, once again the numbers were so big that people on Main Street started to ask questions.

Still the system for these payments continued. Whether or not you agree with these payments is not the problem, the problem stems from the long term damage these payments have on not only the paying entity, but also on every single customer that uses or purchases from these entities.

Does the customer have any say in the size or method of paying a bonus? No, it is the stockholders of the corporations that may make this choice. Simple answer, yet this true answer is also deceiving. All corporations sell a good or service that results in the cash they use to operate. Items like price increases, community involvement or not, and salary limits all add into the bottom line. No corporation would choose to sell a product or service at a price that would not cover the cost of doing business plus a profit margin. Even though the consumer has do direct say in salary limits, they are impacted by all salary decisions. Negotiated increases, health care expenses, all assets and their related costs add into the balance sheets. This puts the consumer in the position of having no vote on what is provided, yet the consumer does bear the expense of being required to pay the cost of goods and services.

The next entry was the cost of employees. The increase in the use of technology began to make people obsolete. Just like ATM's resulted in a reduced number of teller positions needed, changes in many industries made it possible to do more for less, or with less people.

Then it happened, an unrelated event that had far reaching impacts outside the area of the event. 9-11. Businesses scrambled to adjust to the suddenly changed environment they found themselves in. What they did was the right thing to do, managers simply adjusted, quickly, to the immediate change in business conditions. The hotel industry faced a loss in bookings. One manager responded by reducing the number of employees by 324, mostly entry level jobs. This was 2001-2002. The changes and impacts were all new, understood or not, they generally were not questioned. Fast forward to January 2002 and the executive that quickly made the reduction of 324 positions received a $5,000,000.00 bonus.

Doing the math, the bonus closely resembled the same amount the company would have spent if the employee positions had not been eliminated. It was not the money, it was the shot heard around the board rooms. A company can get breakthrough performance by rewarding an executive through the bonus program for actions of the executive. If $5 million could be saved in three months and the business could survive without these positions, maybe there were other positions that could be eliminated. All that was needed was a pay for performance program that would add the cash incentive for company executives.

This change is best described as placing the fox in charge of the hen house. The executive's bonus was directly based on the money the executive could save the corporation. Loyal employees everywhere quickly found out what was really valued by the managers. Loyalty did not count. Neither did seniority, sacrifice, or contracts. The only thing that matters was, what action did the manager need to perform to insure the bonus of the manager.

Wall Street noticed. If a report came out that a company was reducing the number of employees, the stock shot up.

The executive noticed. Hey, this works well. If a manager reduces the number of employees, through whatever means works, the manager exceeds that basic standard and insures an annual bonus. Then, when Wall Street hears about the reduction in force, the manager's 401K or company stock holdings would rise, double bonus. Works for me, the foxes began looking for more hens to slaughter.

Everything and everyone was on the chopping block.

The quick self serving executive then looked at the $3,000,000.00 expense of parts sitting as inventory. Needed or not, the question quickly changed to, can we survive if this figure was reduced or eliminated, and other means of inventory management were used? Once again, with the speed of shipping meeting the needs of business, there was less of a need to have the parts, technology had come to the rescue or should it be said the wallet of the executive? The new standard, became order as needed, when needed, or at failure. Stock on hand did not a bonus make. The executive could simply not buy anything until actually needed, and this would drop to an ability to operate at a lower cost. Operating at a lower cost saved the corporation money, Wall Street was happy and the double bonus standards were achieved, bonus received.

This worked well in year one, but what was the executive to do in year two?
The bonus standards changed, year to year. The fox went on the hunt again.

Customer Service. If Customer Service operations were eliminated, or made more difficult to obtain by moving them to the internet or use of an unending phone tree, less refunds would be paid out. Paying out less to the customer results in better results for the manager, better results allowed the exceeding of year two bonus standards. Operation elimination reduced the expense of equipment needed, reduced the number of employees needed, and reduced the amount of cash refunded. Wall Street noticed, and the double bonus standards were achieved, bonus received.

WOW, folks, there is gold in those darn hills. To the executive it was now time to divide and conquer. It was a new year, with new standards for receiving a bonus, there where sheep to herd! Taking a page from history, the executive looked at departments as yellow badges, red badges, blue badges, etc. The executive would assure the finance department yellow badges, do not worry we are only eliminating the customer service red badges, you are safe. For now.
Calls Centers resulted in the centralization of operations which resulted in no need for local customer service representatives. No need for local representatives, resulted in no need for the building, the equipment, the utilities, this works so well. Executives were floating on cloud nine. The dominos began to fall, where would it be stopped? Department after department, budget line after budget line, everything was now on the chopping block, EXCEPT the bonus. The red badges fell, the yellow badges were eliminated, the cuts went on and on.

What about the consumer? To the executive it was a matter of who signs the check, with the current environment the customer was not signing the check, Wall Street was. Besides the newly empowered executive was faster than the bullet memos used to kill entire divisions, stronger than old leased buildings which were canceled, more powerful than the union agreements which had no opinion, more able to outsource any function or parts of a function without impact and able to shift and shackle the remaining employees with an ever increasing work load. Do not worry, the executive was fearless, the bonus could and would be obtained at any and all cost, fear of loss was for employees, productivity increased. What about the consumer? The who? Stand aside, there is money to be made here.

The Executive became Super-people, the bonus had done exactly what it was intended not to do. Greed had exceeded need, need was viewed as subjective.

Where was this going?

Yes, there was fat, with some of the changes more than likely needed. It all depends on what you need and choose to achieve. Achieving a bonus is nice, but does it add to the overall economy? The answer was overwhelmingly, No.

First the fat was cut, then the surplus was cut, then actual flesh was cut and now with little left to cut, organs deemed not necessary were set adrift. Anything that could be done would be done, all to preserve the bonus and/or company. Companies do longer wanted to strive to be a sole source or the only source, they wanted to be a limited or restricted source for exclusive portions of the market that would insure this new lean mean fighting machine would always generate fat profits and bigger bonuses. Companies no longer wanted to be an economic engine; they all wanted to act like a muffler, catching the parts of business they chose to collect as the air rushed through.

Talking to one executive, the question was asked, if business levels actually came back to the previous levels could you meet the demand? The answer was no, since we have no reserves. We operate on such slim margins, there would be shortages and outages. Then he added, the up side to this is that when business returns in great numbers, this first rush will entirely exceed our capacity to perform, and yet contribute in great numbers to the immediate bottom line. That year the bonus will be tremendous. Greed will never go away, the customer does not matter, the employees do not matter, failure does not matter, the bonus is all that matters. Now that the customer does not matter, customer service is too expensive, so a business system is created to defer the cost of everything by waiting until the item fails, using phone trees to frustrate and defer the phone calls to later or to online, and creating web pages that offer everything in big print, except customer service which is well hidden and requires plenty of input and further wait for any possible action. The customer is not the problem. The business systems seem to have forgotten the truth that the customer is important to any business. Customers need jobs to be customers, who was paying the customer?

Today's phone call was to ask a simple technical question regarding a service offered by a company. Quickly, before any business or questions could be asked, this is after spending 10 minutes getting through the phone tree, the operator insisted that personal information be supplied, so they could serve the customer better. When she was told no personal information would be supplied, as the questions were not of a personal nature and had no bearing on the account, she could not respond. She stated that no further information could be supplied without obtaining specific personal information as she was required to be in compliance with the company rules. A supervisor was asked for. This supervisor insisted that the first and last name be provided in order to continue the conversation. After providing this supervisor the first and last name, a request was made for the supervisor's first and last name. He stated he could only supply his first name. The business standard that applies to the customer is not the business rule that applies to the company. Message received from this was, unless a customer complies with all the rules and regulations of the business, this company does not want the customer. This policy is based on the no one left behind rule, just insure that all customers comply. This company wants no deviation from the company's mission. A non-compliant customer has two options, stay and comply or go away. This company, like many more today, would prefer a non compliant customer just go away, as they only want to serve those customers who are in total compliance. Once the non-compliant customers go away, then this company will be perfect in its mind, as there will be only happy compliant customers providing employee slaves with enough reason to charge the highest and best price for the company to insure the executives are paid the annual bonus. Customers became either the 85% compliant resources, or the 15% please remove this problem person.

As the self serving individuals are in control installing any and all systems that insure the bonus, the evil to the consumer and the shareholders seems to be ignored. Not one penny of a bonus ever increases the bottom line, everything to "earn" the bonus is part of the job description of the bonus earner, so the bonus pays more, for only requiring the employee does the job. Not one penny contributes to the future of the company, as any potential benefit is given away in the larger and larger bonus programs. The consumer, of course, pays for it all. The self serving individual, not thinking of anything but the bonus, always feels the consumer should always pay for the cost of doing business. Bonus payments are passed on to the consumer. Last year's bonus, paid out and not in the company's coffers, requires that in each time period, all costs need to be reflected in the current price. This living in the moment wipes out any legacy or built up benefit. Every service or product is priced in a way that includes all business expenses, including the bonus. This creates the scenario where a company should work hard, have a great product or service they can stand behind, and pass along the lowest/best price to the consumer; instead the work hard, have a product or service that will sell at the highest price the market will allow. Since, the bonus adds nothing to next year's balance sheet the consumer never gets a break. It is pay, pay, pay, so the bonus earner can go play.

Then there is the industry wide excuse of, "We need a good bonus program to recruit and retain excellent talent." What a self-serving and ridiculous remark. If this were true, then no one would ever be able to hire anyone at minimum wage, as there is not enough money offered at minimum wage to recruit and retain an employee. People will work for a reasonable wage, and most do not require a bonus to show up for work. People just want an honest day's pay for an honest day's work. An example, just viewed on a news network, was that of a charitable CEO who retired from the $480,000 per year salary and bonus program she was paid. The charity then searches for and hires a very comparable if not improved version of the retired employee and receives no bonus and gladly accepts the new lower salary. The new employee states the new salary is very generous, a salary of $140,000. The charity saves $360,000 this year. Why did they ever "need" to pay the previous employee $360,000 more per year? It was not required. The pay for performance systems never asks should the bonus be created, the system only states how the bonus program is to be created and paid.

The trap starts when you review who needs to set up and determine the company bonus program. Many of the bonus programs are the responsibility of the personnel department. In most chains of command, the personnel department must create a program that the executives must approve. Seldom is there an independent source used in the creation of a bonus program. The company executives do refer to the fact that their program generally follows industry normal operating bonus programs. This means they liked what they saw, and approved their own salary increase. This socialistic type of doing business does not reflect on the type, quality or size of the company, it points to every business is the same and we should jump on the bandwagon to keep the employee. Communist countries were great in creating a system where the top echelon of workers were compensated by policy and procedural programs. Have good American companies become the new communists?

Why is the question of "should" the bonus system be created not asked, or never allowed to be part of the overall future planning? Most company board rooms do not create the program. The executive office creates the task and delegates the task to a lower level segment of the business. OK, lower level executives, creating, detailing and presenting a pay for performance program.....for their bosses???

Yes, the majority of pay for performance programs are afforded to more than the creators bosses, yet the concept of an employee telling the employer what the employer would be paid, does not create a scenario where the freedom from fear of the employer's response does not weigh heavily on the decisions of the creating authority. Is it possible for any employee, under the direct or indirect control of the employer to make fair and impartial decisions? Most pay for performance creations would borrow from other programs in the market place, and submit these exiting programs as proof of following industry standard compensation programs. Like lemmings jumping off the cliff, company after company chose to accept greed programs without asking why are we jumping.

Future be damned, there is no more important moment than living in the "now".

Take the current part time worker scam. In the past a business would employ five waitresses at 40 hours a week, total of 200 hours per week. These full time employees came with a lot of bonus prevention costs. The full time employee was paid an hourly wage that went up occasionally; there were benefits like insurance and then there was those days off. These employees were keeping the executive from earning a bonus. What to do, what to do? If a company changes the work force from a full time work force to a part time work force, the company found that they could lay off all the higher paid workers. They then could hire new part time workers, scheduling to meet basic coverage and peek times, and reduce overall work hours. These part time workers fall below federal guidelines and benefits like insurance. The company sadly states that the new employee does not qualify for these benefits, as they work only part time. Since most part time workers move on, the company can always find new part time workers willing to work at the lowest possible pay and the company pay basis never goes up.

Brilliant, a slave labor work force that you never need to pay more than the minimum wage, never need to pay for benefits. This increases the executive bonus! The use of the argument which supports the premise that there exists an oversupply of ready to work individuals to keep the part time jobs full at all times; is not applied when referring to the oversupply of ready to advance individuals to fill the executive positions that earn the bonus which, returning to the selfish rule, the bonus is paid to retain or enhance the employment of qualified executives and prevent these enriched individuals from exiting the company for greener pastures. The creation of class warfare by creating over paid controlling business executives at the expense of the masses of underpaid hourly (slave) laborers is not part of the thought process.

Government is not immune to the bonus program payouts. Governments had to create industry standards, or community standards to which the employee had to meet or exceed to "earn" the extra cash for performing their job. The taxpayer never received the opportunity to vote for or against this issue, these were simply personnel issues and not part of the taxpayers area of responsibility. Each year, an employee could earn the basic step increase and/or automatic salary increase as required by union or management agreements, and qualify for an annual bonus payment based on meeting or exceeding performance goals. Oh, I get it. The taxpayer pays the salary plus benefits and the taxpayer pays the bonus! Now the government employee must go to town meeting and proclaim there is a need for tax increases, new fees, increased fees, or all of the above, to maintain the level of service supplied by the responsible government. It had nothing to with service; the government needed more money to cover the bonus cash. Salary cuts, cancelation of the bonus program or a reduction in force never seems to be looked at. A local governmental franchise licensee, a private publicly traded company,

operates and supplies the product/service as contracted through this public service monopoly. The CEO receives a million dollar bonus, after closing customer service offices, applying for and receiving a rate increase; and this bonus was never part of the need for a rate increase submission.

The ability or lack of ability to even talk about the bonus program is legendary. The hush regarding these programs is monumental. No one can ask about, no information is available about, and/or these are private compensation issues that are covered by the privacy laws, are some of the excuses provided. Are they embarrassed by this plundering of the company and/or governmental coffers?

The bonus program and all payroll programs are not considered as part of the overall company/governmental performance. Company after company have been seen dumping higher paid workers only to hire part time or new workers at a new lower pay basis. This reduction in the overall "cost" to the company by the company's own work force is just another factor that contributes to the bottom line while determining the bonus. The message here is clear, if you reduce the cost of employees your bonus goes up. What they cannot justify paying others, they greedily accept as a justified payment to themselves.

Other than an actual owner of a company, executives of any company have always had difficulty in determining the level of pay. For the trustworthy and quality individuals, an honest six figure salary was always acceptable over the bonus program. When the new pay boards entered the scene, and pay for performance programs spread everywhere the check and balance factor of actual honest people making the choice was transferred to other sections. This disconnect resulted in managers saying this is acceptable, rather than feeling any guilt over how these new pay packages compared to the entry level worker. Once the disconnect was in place it became time to obtain the supporting choir. The upper level positions that became part of the pay for performance packages were more than happy to accept these proposals. It is in these positions where most of the down and dirty decisions are made; this is where the shark pool sits. Everyone else were looked at, well "let them eat cake" would be an appropriate statement, as no one receiving a bonus cared. They were now paid not to care, or to be fair. Quickly, the sharks dug into another fat part of the spoils, customer service. Using the safe thoughts of stripping jobs, benefits and demanding higher productivity through fear and intimidation from the work force, they now extended this to the consumer. Customer service was replaced, or removed completely by technology, it is best described by the analyst mantra of " let them obtain customer service on the internet." That comment is as disgraceful as when Marie Antoinette issued her out of contact with the real world "let them eat cake" response.

The downward trend just does not stop. If the pay of employees is reduced, if the number of employees is reduced, if inventory is not maintained or purchased, if preventive maintenance is delayed or not performed at all, if customer service is restricted or removed, if parts of the business are outsourced, if all charitable or community donations or involvement are canceled, all of this and more equates to the increase of executive bonuses. Does a business need to have a social conscience to do the best thing for the customer and the community? Should its businesses only worry about its bottom line and its unique business and contribute only to those causes of their choosing? Is the bonus program the great evil that it has become in the eyes of the consumer?

Somewhere in the middle seems to be the best answer. The best answer could also be that it takes a community to support a business, so support your community by joining charity organizations and by giving back to local causes through sponsorships.

The next wave of reforms is hitting hard at more and more industries. Attending a party last night, a member told of how his world has been turned upside down by the socialist application of Sarbanes-Oxley and the effects on him. He talked about being proud to do a great job, and he was confused about why "his" company is treating a great manager in this new way. He detailed how his job was abolished, and a new job created which only allows those in the company below his level of pay and below the new level of pay need apply. He wondered why they created this new position and why he was being left out. He had used the company's matrix to cut services and positions in an effort to comply with the new rules. Now after accomplishing all that was asked, the company has ignored his "opinion" and wants more for less and from fewer employees. When we talked about the process management system, I stated, " You have no opinion." He sat there letting that sink in, and one could tell the remark had hit home. He was realizing all his efforts, creativity, selfless efforts and contribution no longer mattered. He realized he was now a pawn in a system where the employee needs to comply, survive and be a good team member. Ideas come from the company. His training and experienced were ruled useless and pointless, except if they were used in the fulfillment of the company edict, as written, no changes, alterations or exceptions allowed. You could see the emotions rise, a great American was finally facing the fact that what he was experiencing was a process that he had never thought he would ever experience. He was being confronted with the loss of personal freedoms and liberty, he was also realizing how powerless he was in stopping, altering and modifying this corporate threat.

We talked about how the systems came together to create the bonus led downsizing, necessary cutbacks, or restructuring that had nothing to do with business. It has to do with taking America and the American worker into the third world.

If those at the top of any organization are the only ones that reap the benefits of an enterprise, then you do not have freedom, you have institutionalized slavery. Afraid of losing their life style, department after department, employee after employee fall as victims of the onslaught of this new class of slaves. The working poor are entitled to work, but please do not expect any benefits from that work.

That seems so harsh. With the breaking of the American union movement, business could now dictate the terms of surrender to all the non unionized employees. Once employees were no longer "represented" and were completely alone, who could stand up and make demands? The question should be who would?

A generation of Americans has grown through the last half of the 20th century living life, doing it all and spending like there was no tomorrow. Business systems had pay scales and benefits in place that hard workers could grow and prosper, all by working for a good company. Lives were lived, enjoyed, benefits allowed illness to decrease, retirement seemed like a great future to rely upon. This workforce turned its back on unions or management associations as old , out dated and no longer relevant. Business was taking good care of them, gladly the efforts of these workers made companies very successful, full of innovation, invention, growth and progress. Now with no one and no organization present to protect the worker pay and benefits, business was turning corporate greed loss on all workers. Divide and conquer worked well.

Many companies have weathered the financial changes, finding themselves in a position where expansion and hiring are actually a potential. This is where pay for performance will be put to a real test. What level of sustained sales will prompt the bonus earning gatekeeper to actually allow hiring? First, there will be resistance to hire when the pressure to perform on increased business is applied to a workforce already fearful of losing its job; people will naturally feel that an increased level of productivity will insure their future employment.

History is already showing us that loyalty and legacy are old forgotten concepts when it comes to an executive bonus. Yet, people will perform, over perform and out perform at amazing levels in an effort to earn and preserve their position. The bonus earning executive can sit back and watch his calculator, for as soon as sales increase and expenses (cost of an employee) do not increase, the impact on the bottom line (the bonus) is going to be very high. The efficiencies learned during the business downsizing are equally going to be used and abused during the growth of the economy. If a sales employee must earn $100,000 in sales to "pay" for the position, what level of sales will trigger a new position? Would $200,000 in sales equate to a new position? The bonus earning executive could easily state that sales that only equate to a new position add nothing to the pay for performance bonus. The demands on existing employees to meet and exceed productivity levels of astronomical levels is going to part and the next growth cycle. The executive has nothing to lose if hiring is held off while sales exceed a hiring level, the bonus has a potential of increasing faster than if the increase in sales is offset by the cost basis of a new employee. If the existing sales destroy an existing employee by overworking the individual, well then, the employee will be labeled as one who could not perform to standards, thus shielding the executive. New employees will be held to levels much higher than existing employees as the executive will know that a new employee will be very thankful for actually having a job and will go to great lengths to succeed. Slavery, or institutional slavery, through a business system which rewards the executive at the expense of the employee, is slavery never the less. Asking or expecting the executive to treat employees fairly and equitably in the face of personal greed and opportunity will just not work. Price inflation or market changes that allow for a price increase will not only cover the expense of the product or service, this non-produced/passive increase in revenue will inflate the bonus at no expense in time or effort for the executive. The downward spiral that was so evident in the downsizing of a company to reward the executive will not be reduced or removed when business actually increases, there is simply no incentive to share the wealth (greed). The current generation of executives that created, used and supported the pay for performance programs is not of the persuasion that is concerned, empathetic or thoughtful of the plight of an employee. This current generation is only focused on the bottom line, its bottom line.

What level of responsibility should a business owner take for the pay received by the company employees? Are the social issues caused by earning less than a livable wage a concern for the employer?

Resulting In

Confusion, miss-understanding, dissolution, and anger. Anger began as many people view themselves as hard working pure blood dyed in the wool true blue American citizens. These same people began to blame the current Obama Administration, not seeing or knowing how it was a combination of events, laws and policies that all built up to create the New American socialist state.

Faced with new abilities of this computer age, well meaning local officials are marching in line and in full compliance. The spread of this new socialism is complete.

Yet neither "side" is wholly responsible for what happened and is happening. It seems that private enterprise and government have been caught up in the business approach to operations and employees.

The business side enjoys the increase in employee productivity. Businesses are thrilled by the overall control and flexibility the new systems offer, complete dominant control over a slave-like class of employees, and employees who are comfortable with this level of employee/employer interaction. Governments feel that these new changes are just the next wave and they rush to be good lab rats by seeking immediate and full compliance.

Before we move to the bottom line, which is the results of this new system, where this came from needs to be reviewed.

You cannot hide. The speed of computers and the retention power of storage has created a nasty environment for consumers. The use of a person's credit rating to determine the worthiness of the individual is one area that hurts everyone. If you have an issue with company # 1 and this company reports a negative item to a credit bureau, the individual insurance costs can go up, interest rates on loans can go up and credit card interest rates will go up. The problem with company #1 had nothing to do with the rest of the person's life. Yet the record of this one derogatory report can cost the consumer plenty. One item can ruin a credit rating, require a higher interest rate on any consumer loan, deny the consumer a home to rent, and prevent the consumer from buying a home. Many consumers settle the one item, even though the consumer was correct and the business was wrong, as the pain and cost of standing up for consumer rights does cost more and has more pain than eating one's pride and give in to the demands of a bad business. Business can declare themselves perfectly justified in placing a bad item to a customer's credit rating and at the same time accept no responsibility from the impact this rating has on the consumer. The consumer can do very little, as the business can place an item on a report, be completely satisfied by the consumer, and accept no responsibility for removing the item from the consumer's report.

The use of a arbitrary rating, based on information from business only, that can impact negatively the life and finances of a consumer is just unfair and wrong. When you add in the fact that business is not required to remove items that have been resolved is adding insult to injury.

Labor unions. The labor union movement seems unable to respond.

The changes of pay for performance, job accountability, and the basic right of an employer to insist that all employees work at the direction of the employer has left labor unions failing to respond. When you add on the rush to part time employment, and the lack of rules over this creative abuse of the worker, once again the labor unions either could not or did not respond. The brain washing of an entire generation that has kept the word union in the dirty word category, also went unchallenged. The giants of the American Labor movement are more than likely turning over in their graves as the destruction of the movement is allowed to take place. What the AFL-CIO should have been doing, and/or could have done, will be left for historians to write. The age should surely be labeled as an era when organized labor never recovered after not responding to the body blow provided by the battle of President Ronald Reagan and the firing of the air traffic controllers. The older generation was content, the younger generation accepted this defeat as another reason to not accept a system that seemed and was proving that unions were no longer relevant. When private enterprise unions shrank under the globalization of businesses, the outsourcing of employee needs to non unionized countries, this left public employee unions as a large part of the American unionized workforce. Now, as the Great Recession takes hold and city, county and state governments are faced with lower revenues and constant needs, even these unions are faced with choices. Who really represents the worker, who are faced with the full frontal attack on wages, benefits and jobs? Remember the saying, Stand Together or Die Separately?

Everyone thinks they are a Republican.

The current generation of workers never worried about wages, benefits or retirement. Through the 80's and 90's workers enjoyed the ability to find good employment with good wages. There existed a belief that this period would never end, so the acceptance of the Republican style teachings and beliefs seemed to make perfect sense. Wall Street would take care of the workers' money; companies were growing with ever more opportunities for all who made the right (company) choices, Main street was flourishing; housing was available for all without assistance from any government. It was all about business, business, business. A Republican dream that quickly ended through greed, over control, lack of respect for the worker, total disrespect for the consumer and fraud. The Republican dream began to crash. Yet, even as Wall Street and housing loan fraud were exposed; as workers found out about the evil side of any company which is concerned over the future of the company at the expense of the worker; even as people lost homes by proclaiming what the home buyer did was stupid and what the loan originators did was fraud; the Republican feeling remained. Is the independence of the individual, is the conservative life style of the voter and/ or the feeling of pride and commitment to nationalism simply a Republican theme. The plight of the worker, the ability of groups of people to organize for a common cause and the thought that a worker should be afforded a fair hourly pay for an hour of work did not seem to be a concern of Americans. Most Americans seemed to relate their beloved lifestyle as the Republican dream. People seemed to connect the freedom of internet, smart phones and event attendance as more important than someone other than themselves representing their beliefs. Regardless of how bad the news was, the thought that the results were through the choices of the individual's own creation and not the result of anyone or any other system or action, seemed to be enough for the Republican Party to keep membership. The conservative dream, feed by talk show hosts and the constant reinforcement by political internet traffic; even though more and more Americans began to suffer, the dream remained. People who should believe and align themselves with the Democrats, still feel they are Republican. This too, added to the ability of the new systems to proceed and grow, almost unchallenged.

Drama

Facebook, Twitter, smart phones are all part of this new "connected" world. The constant bombardment of ideas on the average person's email or communication device can lead to informational overload. People begin to tune out certain important items, not because they are less important, because the amount of information, provided from every direction and pointing to every direction can leave a person impotent. Overloaded with thoughts to where one cannot actual decide, and even worse may choose to just go away from the process. Daily, many would love to read the political carton in the newspaper.

Now, the number of political cartoons on the internet is endless, frustration can follow.

Instead of motivating to action, this bombardment seems to numb a person into a political malaise. Not wanting to think about political themes every moment of every day, the average person begins to turn off the process, participate in less causes and live a life of individual personal frustration. Drama may be fun to watch, as reality television ratings point out. Drama is not fun to live with, as it is childish in nature, unending and with no purpose, seldom produces positive conclusive solutions. Yet, we are all faced with making important decisions while suffering through the drama bombardment. Drama seems to be solely created for the benefit of the creator of the drama, hoping to deny a difference of opinion or thought, and to justify the existence or purpose of the drama creator. Drama may create, drama seldom solves or resolves.

Fear

The Greatest Generation was tested by war and survived. Never will I forget after the morning of 9-11 seeing the first veteran and hearing of his attitude and opinion of what happened. There was no fear, just a strong determination that this wrong that had been done was just one act, and that the Greatest Generation retained control and would avenge this attack. Strong determination and quiet reserve to persevere. Action, planned and assured, would insure liberty for all and secure justice for the victims and their families. Confidence that the national systems could and would deliver on their feeling was wonderful to witness. What happened?

As the socialistic changes began to take affect the questions were raised as how could this happen in America. Looking around it became painfully obvious of how it happened.

First, the dummying down of the next generation became a requirement. From 1992 through 2004, the students coming out of high school were not ready to work, were not ready to live on their own and were not ready to defend anything. They could party and procure every device that was created, yet they stood for nothing. An amazing poll asked the 20 something's, what came first, U.S. Law or International Law? 68% stated that International Law came first. This generation was not ready to defend the constitution of the United States. Asking my nephew this type of question, and he responded that his generation would be known as the generation that approved of gay rights, flip flops and moving back home to mom and dad. He continued by saying he did not need to worry about progress as when his parents leave this world he would inherit their wealth. Talking about failures in my family, another parent described the scenario where we provided trophies for all kids, treating all kids the same, we did not reward success, we rewarded everyone wins, and that is simply not the way life is. Her children and mine never had the fear of failure as everyone was the same and everyone wins, how wrong we were.

In the President Reagan years he busted the air traffic controllers' union. Warranted or not, the message that big business received was the door is open for abuse of the worker.

Since 1990, every single year the American worker has lost benefits, jobs, rights and freedoms. The Greatest Generation had new credit cards with a 2% to 3% interest fee that was deductible on your federal tax return. If there was a problem, the bank stepped up with arrangements to help pay the debit without complications. This has evolved to where everyone now faces $39.00 late fees, 24% plus interest rates and reporting plenty of bad information to the credit bureau to drive up other costs like insurance fees , no one steps up to talk about how this problem can be resolved. The Greatest Generation always had each other to rely on, today people have no one. This new system has taken a page from true communism and created the scenario where everyone is held accountable for everything and the banks are not accountable or responsible for what havoc they create and reign over the consumer. Yes, the think tanks knew the Greatest Generation would not accept this new system, so they waited until the Greatest Generation passed on.
This was planned.

So we have the older generation passing on, the younger generation unconcerned, what happened to those in the middle? Think tanks accurately calculated that if the freedom to spend was provided to the masses, then control of the masses would be easy. Personal finances are just that, personal. No one wants to fail, and few admit to their real spending habits. As debit levels went up, and with the approval of the banks, many people where spending beyond their means. When the

47

chickens came home to roost, the consumer found there was no one to help them solve these problems, just a credit rating that was looking worse by the day, bill collectors who treat everyone with great disrespect and with a vile attitude, and the individual's attitude heads south. Faced with all this anger and confusion people, find themselves very alone and afraid. Business interests have done their best to instill in everyone that everyone will be treated separately, no one can get or expect help. The vulture quickly pounces on this fair game.

Fear sets in. People begin to fear losing their jobs; people begin to take any job regardless of how demeaning or low in pay. Families withdraw from social activity and communities begin to see more crime and tragedy. America slips ever so slightly towards the third world.

The fear is a real extension of what happened during the financial meltdown followed by the employment meltdown. When the wage meltdown entered the picture, wage earners everywhere became very aware that current salaries were not guaranteed. Wages were never guaranteed. Since the trend had been for salary increases, when the wind no longer pushed for salary increases, salary decreases came as a shock. As jobs ended and job searches began, the job seeker noticed one very awakening trend, no one was willing to pay anything near the old wage standards, everyone was offering less. Many in the business world would state they had to do this to insure their company could remain in operation. Whether you are a owner or a worker the individual perception of this change was the same, it was sudden and it is permanent.

Now, we have the "generational change" that is being sold to everyone as if this rearranging of the economy is a natural occurring event. Yet, we have bankers and CEOs exiting their businesses with millions in contractual or bonuses that the average worker simply does not receive. We have television commentators stating that people should have known this was coming, that all people should have never taken on more than they could handle, and should never take a job as a permanent situation. It has been stated before, that people taking on too much debt, buying a home beyond their individual ability, is dumb or uneducated. The problem here is the fiduciary responsibility of the company.

Integrity, warranty and corporate responsibility was everything that was preached in America for as long as I can remember. Now customer service was dead, products carried no long term warranty and people began to be treated like targets. In an attempt to push up sales, corporate sales talk began to insure ever single customer was asked if more could be added to the order. If a company could sell more, the company would survive, as for the customer, as a target no one cared, just sell them more. What the customer "chose" to buy, needed or not, was of no consequence to the company, as it was always in the best interest of the company to sell more. There is no better way to sell additional goods or services than to appeal to the customer's fear level. The customer was told they may run out of the product, the warranty would protect the customer, the customer should buy more to insure the customer did not lose out on any advantage real or not real. The sales talk went on and on and on. As sales figures began to grow, this once good idea, became a mandatory speak. Mystery shoppers were used as secret police to insure the employees would work in a climate of fear, fear of not asking the consumer to buy more. If found out to be in non compliance with the sales talk, then the employee could be removed for failing to follow instructions. As employees objected they were quickly reminded that they were employees who were hired and paid to fulfill the request of the employer, employees had no opinion and no choice, follow the script or be removed. Fear for the employee, fear of the consumer, what happened to freedom of choice? The employee has no choice. As an employee there is either do or not do, perform or not to perform, work or have no job, fear worked.

The consumer, or target, was now viewed and talked about by business talks everywhere, as, "It is not your money, you offer the more to buy and the customer decides what and when to buy or not buy, the right to choose belongs to the customer." Many employees knew that the offers of extra service, warranty, and/ or additional product was just sales talk. Many customers knew exactly what they wanted and became vocal about not wanting, expecting or needing this additional sales attempts. The consumer had no say in the process, as managers told employees everywhere, we are just trying to help the consumer, as employees you are required to ask. Respect for the consumer was gone.

The customers did not know what they needed, only the business could know and would offer all the extra services that could be sold would be sold, need was not part of the equation. Fear was on business's side. Employees, consumers, management all learned to live in a culture of fear, fear of doing or losing out. Fear. The outright criminal intent of selling unneeded products through the use of fear was not discussed. It became common practice for a company to ignore the company's fiduciary responsibility in its arena, and take every advantage possible from the customer. What people do may be dumb, what companies do is criminal.

As bonuses and corporate pay increased, bottom line jobs decreased and productivity went up! Yes, people responded to a comply or you will lose out mandate. No one talked to each other, that was dangerous; no one complained, do not want to be known or found out; everyone began to just perform and shut up. Fear of loss had slammed the door on creativity, invention, and interaction. Productivity demands went up, as they were achievable as fearful workers worked more and more as fear of not performing drove many into a frenzy. The people no longer had leadership, the people have become targeted victims, mindless, unorganized, and solitary; any company could now take every advantage possible, no one was challenging the companies, no one was protecting the consumer. The company is accountable to the company bottom line; the company is not responsible for the choices of the consumer, even when marketing an un-responsible response that eventually damages the customer. The company is not accountable for the actions of the customer; the customer is alone and must understand what is being sold to them; the customer must understand that the company is not selling anything, just offering and providing information that additional products or services are available.

Consumer, you have nothing to fear, as long as you purchase more, agree to more and spend more, payday for the company is today, the company is here to drain your bank account, oops serve you. This change in the interaction between the consumer and the company is monumental. Decades of companies supplying the best product or service at the lowest price possible has been replaced by companies willing to sell you the best product or service at the highest price possible, and then add on to this over charging through incidental purchases to insure the health of the company before the health of the consumer. Adversarial relationship to say the least. No longer are companies even trying to hide this new change, in fact they are becoming increasingly brazen in their efforts to first hook the customer and then use foul language, threats of law suits and statements insuring that they will report and ruin the customer's credit rating to reach company goals.

What the heck changed where good brand names would allow this new version of customer "service"? Once again it comes down to a variety of items, not just one item.

Computers are part of it. A company no longer has local customer service agents that actually know their customers. With the absence of local empathy and common ground, a phone center agent and/or online agent can ignore any social or economic reason supplied by the customer and quote the official unchanging computer screen policy. The agent takes nothing personal, it is just company policy; an agent cannot offer or provide any change or alteration to the policy. This, "what part of the written policy do you not understand?" leaves the customer in a difficult position. The customer has personal reasons for problems, not all customers are exactly the same, and sometimes everyone needs a little time to straighten out personal matters. Companies today do not care, as the new corporate belief is customer service for their customers is expensive; allowing agents to have authority to offer relief to their customers is expensive; any delay in the collection of service fees is expensive; and relief from the excessive late fees is very expensive. Any expense does not add to the company bottom line, and it is company bottom lines that create and pay the massive bonuses paid to the corporate elite. The customer no longer mattered.

Companies large and small have come to the conclusion that 85% of their customers are, what the company defines as company's marketing resource databank. If a company "mines" the list of the consistent paying, no problems, no interaction with customers, then the company can drive profits which drives the bonus. The remaining 15% are expendable. Please correct your own problems, pay the company more and more, and then just go away. We have reached the age where the demographics of the population have made the customer lack of service policy possible. Corporate America has made the choice to serve for a fee, the 85% of the population that creates profits at the lowest possible cost for the other 15%, corporations respond with a policy that states, companies are not responsible for customers who, through their own personal choices, find themselves in a difficult or impossible situation. All customers are expected to accept, understand and follow the company's rules of service; just remember the customer is a financial asset of the company and is expected to serve the company without opinion, problems or any need beyond the service requested and supplied by the company.

The customer is screwed.

Customers need service, yet they also need an attorney to read and understand the company policy that is included in all transactions. Consumers had become attached to the internet, smart phones and satellite television, so they shut their mouths, paid the bills whether agreed to or not, as it became better to have a perceived lifestyle than to shut off a cell phone and be found out as one who was doing so well. Fear, combined with keeping up with the Joneses, results in fear of failure; a forced compliance lifestyle.

People now serve business. A country of, by and for people is in danger. Business through these tactics of fear and intimidation taught the consumer all about compliance with a policy. Government plans to keep people right there, in fear and in compliance.

Is this the era of the Death of the Individual?

Death of the Individual

Accountability and personal accountability became the hallmark statements or requirements of the new systems. The computer could be used to spread the processes to every retail location with the same message and insure continuity. The focus could be placed on the lowest performing sites, demanding a level of compliance, obtainable or not, that was set by the home office. Driving performance through a system that sets standards and confirms and having these standards met or exceeded by all sites was a major breakthrough. The control over every section of the company was now firmly in the hands of the CEO. Reports could now be created, updated and reviewed daily. These reports are used to see trends, patterns, failures and results. Success of a unit or a person was not longer important. Individual performance was now overshadowed by the "team" concept.

Your team became the vehicle that was to be trained, and retrained, and retrained to achieve the demands of the organization. No one individual was important, everyone was judged as all achieving the results or all failing to achieve. There were now team meetings that consist of spreading the company ideals and propaganda to everyone.

Managers quickly found their usefulness and authority was disappearing, as once everyone is trained to be a manager, there would be no need for a manager. Systems obliterated the need for a manager, just read the screen and follow the instructs, no more, no less. What part of what is on the screen needs a manager?

Customer service was shifted to a call center. This shift reduced the need for managers, and dropped the level of education needed at retail outlets. If a front line clerk was only required to read the screen and follow instructions, the level of sophistication required for all locations could be reduced. The manager's authority and decision making responsibilities were replaced by the standard operating procedure requiring referral of all items not on the screen to the call centers. Local flavor could be eliminated and or never considered as this local flair had no place in the corporate one size fits all mentality. Local managers could be eliminated or downsized as their level of importance to the company had diminished. If manager and employees could be trained to follow a team concept of procedures, then the risk to the company would be reduced. Besides, the customer loved and expected the same experience at every single location.

"Failure to follow instructs", could be used as the catch all reason for removing any employee. Failure to meet or exceed standards would be used as a way to determine that the manager or unit was failing to follow instructions by not meeting or exceeding performance standards. The performance standards is all that counts; the people did not, location did not, the company mandates as determined from above were always correct. Since the company never admits to mistakes, ownership of errors could now be shifted to exact non-performing locations or products. The board was firmly in control of the company; individual effort by any one person outside of the boardroom had no specific impact on results. Teams or locations either meet or exceeded standards which were determined as required by the board room, and the accountability systems were in place to report the results. All success or failure ownership was placed on the team or location. The individual performance, where stars are created, was no longer needed, or rewarded. Star performance by an individual is seen as potentially harmful, as the unit could and would suffer if this star ever left the section. This upward or downward movement of a section was not what personal and unit accountability was all about. If the performance was based on one star performer then the system would suffer at some point in time. If the performance was based on the entire unit workforce, then the dramatic ups and downs caused by individual star performance could be eliminated. A steady progression towards meet or exceed the business standards was all that was required. No company needed star players, every company wanted team players. The individual was no better or worse than the entire reporting unit. Every employee of the team either supported the team or failed to follow instructions to support the team. An individual either fit in with or did not fit in. If an individual did not fit in, well, then that one person had to go, that one person was not in compliance with maintaining and working with the team concept.

Star performance was not acceptable, as it was no longer acceptable that certain individuals could and would exceed performance standards, while the majority would not. Everyone was expected to learn and perform to corporate standards; individual ability to excel did not matter. The team concept is not like a relay team where there are team members who provide the best performance when they are running their leg of the race. When you combine the best performance by the individual runners you take each leg of the race and a winner is declared to the team with the best overall performance. Usually the last runner, who either added to or subtracted from the overall performance of the previous runners who did their part and then passed on the baton, crosses the finish line first, the winner. The new team concept is much more socialistic. Now, the four man relay race would be run quite differently. The new team race has all four runners starting out at the same time, at the same place. All four runners are expected to run at the performance standard pace, through each leg of the race, always tied together. Then it is further expected that all four runners cross the finish line, together, all at the same exact time. The team won, the individual lost, there were no individual efforts, there was a win based on teamwork. Individuality would not be rewarded, the individual was dead. Sounds like socialism to me.

In the 1990's, when sports teams gave trophies to every team player, instead of just the star performers, we signed on to this program. In using the no child left behind in our schools, we ignored the students who just went away. Many school counselors, in order to meet the schools' performance standards, will suggest to poor attending and poor performing students, to leave. Join the Army, go out and get a job, the student is not helping the team, so go away, so those remaining can be viewed as a team that has met or exceeded the no child left behind standards. Schools, companies, governments took the stance that they are no longer responsible for the individual, only accountable to the standard. Those outside the line are best served by just being outside of an organization, as the individual is viewed as the problem. Darwin's Theory of Evolution is thrown out, natural happening mutations are deemed as dangerous and unmanageable, not as the necessary change that insures the survival of the species. The people who can leave their unique individuality at the door and work at the industry standard are acceptable, those who cannot separate their individuality from their work performance need not apply.

This separation of the classes in schools and the work place creates the scenario where the new standard of living is based on just two separations, the haves and the have-nots'.

It could be argued that this process just speeds up the natural selection process. Most people do leave most of their unique individuality at the door, or go off in pursuit of those individual interests anyway. The problem with this new team concept reality, is the institutionalizing (socialism) of the concept. Natural selection has been replaced by institutional compliance. This is an attempt to remove all risk and to insure the bonus payments for the upper level of the institution.

The individual at entry level is viewed as a person who chose not to educate themselves to the level that would require this person to be applying for this entry level position.

Therefore, no responsibility is extended over or accepted for this person's failure to achieve. A company is free to insure all entry level workers, regardless of length of service, loyalty to the company, are compensated at the lowest pay possible. The bonus must be protected; if you pay others there is no money left to pay a bonus.

The use of company sharks, persons who would sell their soul for advancement, feeds into the process without regard to self or the other people. Sharks demand results, will move anywhere to tend to the sheep, holding a vision that lists themselves as number one, and the rest of the world as cannon fodder. The use of people as a tool, technology as a control and self-grandizement as a fuel, leads towards a goal that disrespects or ignores the lives of employee and customers. Incentive buy solicitations, all consumers are game for the hunting, and the company is not responsible for the customers bottom line, the community's needs and/or society advancement and everything or anything else are an addition to or a detriment to the company's bottom line. These sharks may be able to meet a personal short term goal, they do not take responsibility for the world around them.

Accountability and the required compliance are not traits of a free society. Realize that accountability and compliance is socialism. The centralized form of management is a socialist model, all for one and that one is not you. that one is the centralized business or government. Both business and government say that this centralization is being done to better serve you; it is what they are not saying and what they are not doing, that has become the problem. The individual and individual effort was deemed uncontrollable and problematic. Through the issuance of standard operating procedures and the centralization of services, the risk of a real individual/rogue employee was reduced.
Risk assessment and risk mitigation, sounds like the intent of Sarbanes-Oxley helping to reduce the role of individual performance.

What we need to do

Be an individual.

Do not be afraid to be independent.

Do not be a sheep

Be an American

Organize, join others, you are not alone

Stay FREE! and live.

By being an individual, a person can grow in the understanding that this empowers the person towards freedom. You were born alone, you are not part of the crowd and you must insist on being treated like the person you are. Individuals live their lives independent of the system, just like the legendary Harley riders. It was their independence and individuality that brought millions to support the cause. Yes, buy a Harley!

Buy locally. If all politics are local, so should all your financial decisions. When you visit the "mom and pop" stores you are providing cash to where your community needs it most. Local owners spend money in your community, support local causes and reinvest those monies locally.

These local businesses generally hire more people and pay better than the larger corporate concerns. Locals do not have a set spending plan sent down from corporate with orders to follow the plan regardless of conditions. These independent operators have the flexibility to raise or lower prices; to hire full or part time; as the markets dictate. They can turn on a dime as it is an incentive to them to do so, since they do not have the need to wait for a corporate decision, this response can lead to greater profits and more local improvement. Local owners are members of a local church, a local charity, a local club. These are the people who support the local sports teams, show up at local events and buy tickets to everything local. This entire "buy local" process provides the cash that drives the local economy. Having a vibrant alive local economy creates an environment where more business and business opportunities are created. Cash that stays in the community rotates around town and keeps everyone working. When corporations took over main street only to obtain market share, then withdrew to call centers, it took the life line out of the community. Prices went up, service went down and jobs were lost. Buying from locals has all the opposite effects. You can call and get a task accomplished, quickly, efficiently and with the intent to serve, they live here too.

The local businesses know that you talk, so they serve you to get the good news spread, not that ho-hum corporate response, this is as good as it gets. Local businesses know they can increase their business by taking care of their customers. You are not just another number, you are important.

Stay Free. Under bureaucratic laws such as Sarbanes-Oxley, the individual loses everything. The individual is supposed to read and perform; what part of what is written does the individual not understand? Failure to follow instructions become more important than, How may I help you? Signing or initialing a form to "prove" compliance with a policy or practice is just sick. This blanket compliance with the written word treats everyone as guilty first until proven compliant, with all rules known and unknown, understood or not understood. This crucial part of the communistic like manifesto is insidious at best. This is where the battle line must be drawn; choose freedom over compliance control. How does one stay free?

If you do not need to do so, do not do it. Your approval of, signature of acknowledgement of, initialing of a form for the store to be in compliance, is not the practice of free people. Just say NO. If this means you must go to another business that does not require these corporate policies, then go. You must choose between freedom or compliance; choose to be free. Everyone cannot and does not learn, absorb or comprehend everything at the same rate or in the same time period. To place this expectation upon everyone and everything is for purposes of control and compliance, this has no place in a free society. People are different, and in this difference there exists the unique qualities that sometimes blend and sometimes cannot blend, yet make up a very vibrant, alive and diverse society. In this diversity there is freedom, freedom of individual expression and growth of the individual. In Compliance there is an attempt to treat everyone as the same, to paint all the individual qualities, those personality quirks that make us all special, with one boring gray brush. Compliance shuts off life, kills invention, creativity and smothers inspiration. Allowing diverse individuals to be an individual insures this society will grow, prosper and change for the good of the people. Being and remaining an individual is the first step for a free society. Watched a television show where the government moved 8 year old girls away from their families to schools where the girls could learn how to have a better life by complying with the discipline rules to provide a team approach where all people move as if one, for the betterment of the state, forget who you are. This teaching of everyone can succeed if the individual forget themselves and "unselfishly" performs for the good of the state, is pure socialism. This process also does not allow the freedom of self expression, the freedom to think differently to invent, the group can overrule any innovation deemed not in compliance with existing norms and ignore the diversity of the population.

You are not a slave! If a computer calls you, hang up. You are not required, nor is your self-esteem so low, nor is there any law that requires you to sit there and wait for a computer to connect you to anyone. Your time is just as valuable, if not more valuable than the cost of the low paid operator on the other end of the line. A person calling for a doctor's for an appointment, the message said leave the name, birth date and phone number, they would get back to the caller! So, they expect you to sit there all day waiting patiently for their over worked under paid attendant to find the time to return the call. Many businesses are purchasing these "new" call management systems. To get to the point where the message could be left, required that the customer listen and then push #2 four times, to be told to leave a message. Who is in control here? If any office is so busy there is not time to answer the phone, then hire an employee. Instead companies purchase a system and rely on the fact that their existing employees will find the time to return all calls, at the employee's convenience, not yours. This office has been visited many times before, observing the employees, while waiting an average of 1.5 hours after the appointment time. These employees do not answer the phone, have plenty of down time and must be waiting for the end of the day to make all the calls at once. You are not being treated like the valuable customer that you are, their fees have not gone down, the level of customer service has dropped to zero. The business system that creates these products does not sell customer service, they sell employee time savings to the company. Saving time is saving wages, there is never a sales pitch that informs the buyer that if this system is purchased, the company's customers will suffer, will be treated like the customer does not matter.

You matter, it is your cash that is keeping this company in business. Yes, they are busy, yes they are over worked, yes they need to review their problems and solve their problems. To say that solving their time constraint problem is completed by dumping the problem over to the customer is just wrong. Sure there is a need for an appointment, remember you are important, your time is important, you are not a slave. It took five calls to finally get through to a real human to make an appointment, cost of the calls was five minutes, time between the first call to the last call, seven and one half hours. Your seven hours and twenty five minutes are valuable, sitting by the phone that long just hoping and praying the company would return the call is just sick.

Customer bill of rights:

You are a human being, independent and an individual.

You are not a sheep, to be herded and corralled.

You are not required to be a team player, you are unique and have unique abilities that are not rewarded by a team concept.

You are not required to have call waiting, an answer machine, or a cell phone.

You are not required to wait for a computer to connect you to an operator.

You are not required to listen to a computer tell you anything.

You are not required to have any calls recorded, unless you agree.

You do not lose your rights because you disagree with a company policy.

You are not required to guess at what was just stated, tell them to slow down and repeat what they are saying until you understand.

You are not required to listen to any sales pitch for any product or service.

You never agree to sign any privacy policy form unless the form is reviewed and found acceptable by your attorney.

You are not required to be in compliance with any company rule or procedure.

You are the customer, if you do not like what it happening, leave.

You choose where to spend your money, say no to Madison Avenue marketing.

Remember ME, I am your customer. This statement should be remembered to keep you from being used, abused and refused.

What do good customers do when treated with a lack of dignity and respect? Good customers, just go away.

Nothing on this earth is needed so badly that should require individuals to give up their freedoms just to be in compliance with a computer, a system or a company's lack of customer service. When you follow this mantra, you will find better companies, have much less stress and the message to the business will be, the customer is king. You work hard for your money, provide it willingly to companies that serve you. Never fall into the trap of serving company needs before the company provides you a product or service.

Make them remember you as their customer, or inform them that you WERE their customer.

Complain. Use whatever form there is available, phone, email, fax, or a letter. Most companies found out that as they required people to visit FAQ (frequently asked questions) first, or sit through obnoxious phone trees, many complaints just went away. The fine art of demanding a certain level of business is part of being in business. The feedback from an angry customer keeps out of touch managers honest. They are required to answer, as you have made them responsible for their response. Written emails or letters will be filled with corporate premeditated horse manure, but it is a start. Fire back and demand an answer to your specific concern and do not let a company off the hook until they provide the service you paid for. Use the documentation they keep on you by keeping the documentation on them to accomplish your goal.

Be Prepared. Answer the phone or when a person finally answers you, please be ready. Write down and follow the bureaucratic rule:

If it is not documented, it did not happen.

Write down the date and time of the call.

Write down the phone number you called.

Ask for a call back number.

Write down the representative's name, ID number and/or location.

Obtain a case number, if possible

Write down what the representative states will be done to resolve the problem.

Remember, if it is not documented, it did not happen.

Be responsible, there is nothing that can guarantee your rights, if you choose to make choices that are not sustainable. All the consumer protection laws will NOT stop a person from making a bad choice. Be responsible to educate yourself, so you know before you sign on the bottom line.

Is It a Security Issue?

It is a matter of compliance so a system can make it safe for everyone, the flyer states. How do you find a needle in a hay stack? Every airline passenger would agree that there should be every precaution to prevent any violent action from taking place on an airborne plane. So is surrendering your privacy and freedom worth a person's safety and security? The balancing of freedoms and security is a very difficult and potentially controversial topic of discussion. It is hard to think of anyone who would refuse to follow security procedures and by doing so, risk their life. Does this mean that the terrorists won? Personal freedoms have been reduced, brought on by terrorist activities. The terrorists achieved their goal through acts of terror; we all live in fear, and now we all suffer through security procedures. Repeating, no one would ever really have an issue with safety and security procedures. There needs to be a balance and there needs to be discussion. If technology can replace removing shoes at an airport, then removing that specific procedure should be the end result. The ability to increase a procedure must be balanced with the same ability to remove a procedure. It is a bureaucratic fear of failure that retains too many procedures, laws and regulations on the books. A free and independent board of citizens could serve the purpose of being a check and balance approach to the bureaucratic retention of procedures. Free people will always make better decisions than employees who are worried about their source of continued employment.

Organize.

First organize yourself. A house divided against itself cannot stand. Review where you spend your money and why and where you earn your money and why and where you save your money and why. If your mutual fund is not performing look around, talk to people, find a local CPA, and make the moves necessary to improve performance. Please do not stay with a bad fund just because it takes effort to move the a different fund. Savings account pay next to nothing, so pay yourself first. Take the 1% the banks pay, and each month you add another 6%, from your cash, the rate of return will then be 7%; your funds will grow and be safely insured. Create a number of funds that expire on different dates, so you can keep control and review each account periodically.

Next, where do you spend your money? $4.50 coffee at a branded name store, or $1.49 coffee at a local convenience store? Find the better price with the same style of product and save daily. Stop eating lunch out every day, there is nothing wrong with a brown bag lunch except your co-workers will know you are saving money. Practice the concept of, on days off or while out shopping, waiting until you get home to eat, you save time and you save cash. If you really want or need to dine out, always choose a locally owned establishment. Remember, these local stores offer better food at good prices, and the money stays in your community and is not funneled to Wall Street. Tip heavily, we are long past the days of the one dollar tip. The new standard should be leave them $5.00 to help keep them alive. Tips are local money being spent locally, with approximately 65% spent each day. This free exchange of cash can and does stimulate local economies, as it provides funds to local people and away from Wall Street.

Talk to your fellow workers to keep up with what is really happening. Use the governmental resources like the Department of Labor to report any and all pay issues. Know what others are earning, and seek a higher wage. Join political campaigns, as when you work for others you increase your ability to have your real concerns listened to.

Understand risk. The use of the theory surrounding the knowledge of and the mitigation of these known and unknown risks, may seem sound. The reality of risk is that risk is directly connected to the human factor. As long as you have humans performing tasks, creating systems and being involved in a process, risk will not be mitigated or removed. Yes, the systems try through a series of ongoing system reviews to remove or mitigate all risk as soon as it develops or becomes known. Upon discovery of a new actual, potential, or perceived risk; that the downward tightening of the screws, creates a life destroying environment. With each tightening of policy, the system begins to work like a boa constrictor, slowly and effectively squeezing the breath out of the victim.

The victim is the consumer. The tightening process also destroys beyond the actual intended victim. As others hear of the process, there is the natural risk avoidance, pain avoidance reaction that takes place. Others, who have only heard of the pain, simply stay away. This reduction in business activity, as a direct result brought forth from the business system designed to limit risk and increase profits, actually decreases opportunity to create profits. The company then responds by labeling another part of the company as risk, downsizing and layoff follow. We then reach the level being experienced by many, many parts of business and industry, the entire interconnected system becomes constipated.

Nothing moves. The screws are just too, too tight. All breath has been squeezed out of the victim, the compliance officers are standing by waiting to pounce on any sign of life, the consumer is either too scared, frustrated or angry to even leave the house. It is like when the body shuts off the blood flow to the arms and legs, to save the heart and brain, when in reality the controlling parts cannot live without the entire body. Activity cannot and should not be accepted as progress.

In Conclusion

This book was written not to include specific data and information that would quantitatively prove any and all statements or presumptions of this author. The facts have grown to such a large proportion of corporate life, that singling out one item would be fruitless. This book was written from a stand back and look what has happened to us all. Our freedoms and liberties have been crushed not by one source, not from any foreign force, and while everyone thought the action that was being taken was the correct action item to provide, protect and defend all.

Quite the opposite. This perfect storm required the master chef's touch of adding all the ingredients into play in order to achieve a new perfect taste. There was no master chef or proponent for this action, it was the blending and naturally occurring random acts or facts that combined in light of a full sun, to create a realm of darkness and gloom. The authors and approvers of Sarbanes-Oxley never imagined that this simple law could and would create such a negative situation where personal freedoms of the general public, companies and our collective futures would suffer.

The sum of the equation is the product of all the parts of the equation. This destruction of the a free independent America, home to free individuals, and with a government of the people, by the people and for the people became the victim of many processes.

Was it the computer and the new massive capabilities of this products, yes but not alone.

Was it the lawyers and their quest to rule and control the world, yes but not alone.

Was it Sarbanes-Oxley, the law that needs to be repealed quickly, yes but not alone.

Was it fear, yes but not alone.

Was it process management, yes but not alone.

Was it Wall Street greed, yes but not alone.

Was it the need of governments to raise cash, yes but not alone.

Was it the need to protect the citizens from any risk foreign, domestic, known, not known, yes, but not alone.

It takes two to tango, here it took many people, actions, processes, rules, regulations, laws, actions, inaction, time and fear to create the ending of a free America. It is truly believed that no one person, company or foundation could ever have had this process and the end results as the intent of a plan. Nothing could ever have worked this well, formulated with this specific intent. Intent had nothing to with this. The proper way to describe this is the word, able.

Politicians created Sarbanes-Oxley with the intent to mitigate corporate risk, once on the books other used the law for their own intentions because they were able to do so. The government incorporated the law into every thought and action of company, individual and corporations because they were able to do so. Everything came together not through the effort or lack of effort of any one or any group of individuals. This process took on a life of its own, because it was able to do so.

The American individual needs to make a decision. Do you want to be free? What cost do you want to pay to provide the level of freedom that we once enjoyed in this country?

There are many who are doing just fine, as the cash flow and freedom they enjoy is based on their place in life. Many others have not found or are still seeking the answer to "what should I do with my life?" Both seem to have the major focus on money, what money can and cannot do based on what they have or do not have. Instead of finding their passion, they allow their passion to be consumed by the day to day fight for existence. This was never more evident than the last election where it seemed that 47% are doing just fine and 47% are not, with 6% still undecided.

Business seems to keep people working and confident, from the owners view point. As an employee, the past gains of the organized workforce spread through many non organized employment bases. The current model is based on a new generation of business owners who do not respect, care for or want to provide anything for their employees. When you take the minimum wage and reduce this by the cost of health care, uniforms, inflation, etc., you have people bringing home much less than they have in the last 50 years. The business owner sees governmental fees going up, compliance rules and costs escalating, generally the cost of doing business rising every day; they too are bring home much less than they have in the last 50 years.

Wall street is doing just fine. They always loved making money off some else's money, and never seem to worry about the suffering on main street.

To this writer it all comes down to the individual, and the individual effort. No one was going to put these thoughts into a book except through the individual efforts of the writer.

No one is going to vote, save money, find a new career, stop buying spontaneous items, and learn to just say no, without individual effort, or shall it be said, a little intestinal fortitude. The use of the team concept, has lead to where everyone thinks they can win, without first figuring out that at what level of winning can they achieve from where they stand. An example's is the student who places all hope on a scholarship, and little faith on working, saving and a plan. We all seem hooked to the dream, rather than focusing on the journey towards a dream. We all need to get back to reality, get our head out of Wall Street and Washington DC; and focus on our hometown, where we work, where we play, where we live. Sure we can escape for a weekend at a fancy resort, yet if the cost of that weekend comes at the expense of a future dream like college expense, the immediate emotional response is not the best choice.

It all comes down to individual choice, not emotional response.

We must remember we are human, and those we deal with are humans. Resist the business systems that try to root out all risk, as life itself is risk. Systems like these create a program that takes on a life of its own and ignores the real lives that are impacted by the program. Every person who supports a system over the human, becomes part of the problem. The problem is a system that is not forgiving, not flexible and too controlling.

It is through this control that a system can harm humans without any malice, it is just that the system does not leave any wiggle room for real people. People are not perfect, people are not always in compliance, people are emotional, people make mistakes, people are our brother and sisters in this world. A system does not forgive, does not give discounts, does not allow for error, does not stop demanding and ignores the actual humans that provide the system with actual life. Empathy for life, not everyone learns at the same pace, not everyone understands, not everyone knows what the system needs. Every year the world receives the lives of a fresh batch of sixteen-year-olds, who know nothing about life and need real people to help them learn. It is our job to teach, educate and also, to forgive and love people. The robotic response required by a business system is what should be feared, as when a system does not support life, then the system begins to destroy the essence of what it is to be human. We cannot have or expect the perfect risk free system where customers are always available and profits are always high, while the risk and expense of employing humans is reduced to the lowest possible level. Not everyone needs to know and needs to understand what it takes to repair a car, that is the job of those people who love automobile repair, and seek and learn that area of knowledge. When our car needs repair, these are the humans we seek out and pay for their service. Some people cannot read frequently asked questions and perform self diagnostics to repair the car; no, some people just want to turn the key and drive.

To really succeed in this world, one needs to take care of people, those in our lives, those who walk or run through our lives, those whom we love, those whom we never meet. We cannot and should not try to replace people, for in this attempt to remove all risk, we are trying to remove all people. This is not love: this is control, this is inhuman, this is not life. The choice is ours; choose people and treat them with love. In an adult state economy, versus a daddy state, or a mommy state, choosing responsible sustainable actions with maximum consideration for people is essential to success.

Systems are all about making money, life is all about people, choose people. Life is not about greed, personal wealth, life is about what you do for others, not to others.

Business and government are sick. There is no love and no life in a business system, and when you strip away the fluff that covers these systems, all that is left over is, Greed.

Bible verse states, love is kind. Be kind to people-yes, to business and government, take the lead of President Harry Truman and give them hell.